Alcohol
Controlling the Toxic Spill

By Michael deCourcy Hinds

Introduction

Excessive drinking creates countless personal disasters, including job losses, bankruptcies, suicides, divorces, crimes, lost friendships, and ruined family life. Nearly one in ten adults meets criteria for chronic alcohol abuse or alcohol addiction, and one in four Americans feels the pain caused by alcohol problems. How can a democratic society safely control the drug alcohol? As with other NIF issue books, this one provides an overview of the issue and, to promote public deliberation, outlines several perspectives, or choices. Each choice speaks for one set of American priorities and views and, drawing ideas from across the political spectrum, advocates a unique and consistent approach to the issue.

Choice 1 Demand Citizen Responsibility

Most Americans enjoy alcohol and use it responsibly in compliance with laws. Today's problem is that our halfhearted enforcement of alcohol control laws not only makes a mockery of law and moral order, but actually encourages underage drinking as well as irresponsible and illegal alcohol use. To deter alcohol abuse, the nation must draw the line on the irresponsible use of alcohol and provide swift, certain, and severe punishment to those who cross that line.

Choice 2 Treat the Public Health Epidemic

The abuse of alcohol is not a law enforcement problem, but a public health epidemic that the practice of medicine can best cure. Alcoholism itself is a disease, often inherited, that is shrouded in stigma, confusion, denial, and ignorance. In this view, many more programs for prevention, early detection, counseling, and treatment are needed to address the range of alcohol problems leading up to and including addiction.

Choice 3 Educate for Societal Change

Progress in enforcing laws or in curbing an epidemic will remain elusive until Americans personally confront the problems of alcohol abuse – much the way they did with smoking and cancer. Using the antismoking campaign as a model, this choice calls for society-wide educational efforts to dispel falsehoods and ignorance about alcohol and, at the same time, generate popular social norms and public policies for responsible behavior.

Alcohol
Controlling the Toxic Spill

CORBIS/Bettmann

The name of the game here is getting drunk on spring break. Many Americans, especially the young, drink excessively with little regard for the health and social consequences.

It was "Senior Week," the annual blowout dreaded by parents and dreamed about by graduating high school seniors in metropolitan Philadelphia. Senior Week, which over the years has evolved into a rite of passage, disperses unchaperoned teenagers to seaside towns for a week of partying and living dangerously. But on June 28, 1998, the *Philadelphia Inquirer* gave parents new cause for anxiety.

Datelined Cancún, Mexico, the front-page story began with a blunt warning: "If your daughter or son is in this primo party town for Senior Week, you may want to stop reading." The article reported that of the 200,000 American teens partying in Cancún, at least 1,500 were area youths, drawn by the cheap tours (a complete "party tour," including unlimited alcohol for seven nights, cost $750). Miles of beaches, numerous bars, and a rarely enforced legal drinking age of 18 all contributed to the sport of getting drunk and out of control. The *Inquirer* described a typical scene at Señor Frog's bar: "Girls sitting atop bouncers' shoulders pour tequila into the mouths of drunken teens below. The first girl to pour the whole bottle wins; the losers have to drink what's left in their bottles." From her poolside lounge chair, Adrienne Saccone, 18, of Holy Spirit High School in Egg Harbor Township, N.J., observed: "Everyone is drunk all day and all night." Her friend, Andrew Allen-Aguilar, 18, of Austin, Texas, added, "It's horrible the things that go on here, but I love it."

Andrew's candid ambivalence about alcohol abuse is shared by adults – and goes a long way toward explaining why the nation has trouble facing its drinking problems. A second reason is the nature of the beast: it is hard to be clear about something that spans healthful drinking, social drinking, youthful binge drinking, irresponsible drinking, and alcoholism. Finally, the issue never seems to get the attention it deserves, perhaps because society tends to focus on the individual problem drinker and not the great forest of suffering. Alcohol abuse takes a heavy toll on America, damaging public and private life with countless traffic fatalities and injuries, home fires, drownings, suicides, violent crimes, bankruptcies, ruined careers, suicides, divorces, birth defects, and children with permanent emotional scars. Directly or indirectly, these and other drinking-related problems touch one in four Americans.

But how does a free society cope with something like alcohol? It is at once a civilized food and an addictive drug. About 100 million adults use it legally, setting role models for illegal use by 11 million minors – and nearly 14 million meet criteria for chronic abuse or addiction. Historically, alcohol bears ancient links to victory and tragedy, health and sickness, religion and crime. With such an array of opposing forces, and no easy answers for reducing alcohol abuse, it's human nature to look on the bright side and stoically accept the dark side. But as more researchers, social scientists, and physicians examine the problems, new discoveries are informing public discussions, infusing them with fresh optimism – and greater urgency.

How can the nation approach today's problems with alcohol abuse? As with other NIF issue books, this one provides an overview of the issue and, to promote public deliberation, outlines several perspectives, or choices. These approaches may overlap in certain aspects, but each choice speaks for one set of American priorities and views and, drawing ideas from across the political spectrum, advocates a unique and consistent approach.

Better Understanding

Today drinking is an accepted fact of American life, serving social functions and satisfying personal appetites. Most Americans enjoy alcohol without any problem. And science pours out studies implicating alcohol's toxic effects and lauding its health benefits. There's good news for those who drink lightly or moderately (the government's 1995 nutritional guidelines define "moderate" as no more than one drink a day for women and no more than two drinks a day for men, based on differences in body weight and water content): scientific evidence shows that moderate consumption of alcohol can reduce cardiovascular disease among middle-aged and older men and postmenopausal women.

Other good news is that since the 1980s Americans have been drinking less, resulting in correspondingly lower rates for associated problems. For example, alcohol-related traffic fatalities fell to 16,189 in 1997, a 6 percent decline from 1996. Although these fatalities still accounted for a whopping 38.6 percent of all traffic deaths, it was the lowest rate since the federal government began keeping records in 1975.

But bad news abounds. Research, much of it sponsored by the National Institute on Alcohol

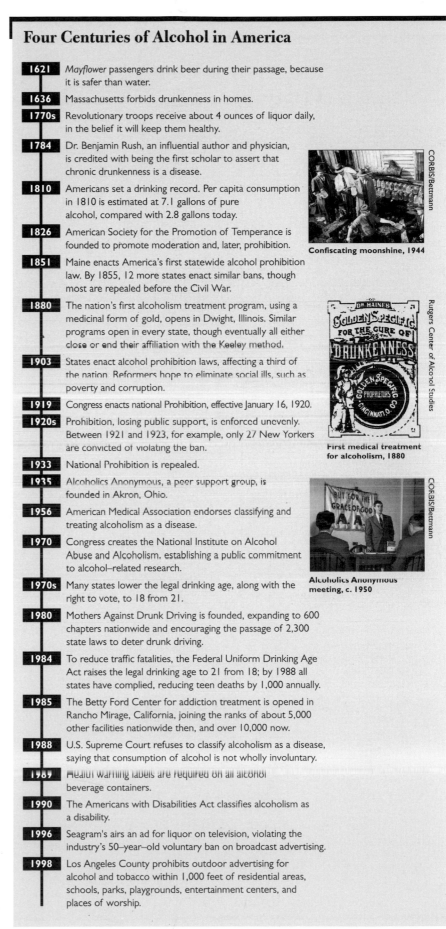

Four Centuries of Alcohol in America

1621 — *Mayflower* passengers drink beer during their passage, because it is safer than water.

1636 — Massachusetts forbids drunkenness in homes.

1770s — Revolutionary troops receive about 4 ounces of liquor daily, in the belief it will keep them healthy.

1784 — Dr. Benjamin Rush, an influential author and physician, is credited with being the first scholar to assert that chronic drunkenness is a disease.

1810 — Americans set a drinking record. Per capita consumption in 1810 is estimated at 7.1 gallons of pure alcohol, compared with 2.8 gallons today.

1826 — American Society for the Promotion of Temperance is founded to promote moderation and, later, prohibition.

Confiscating moonshine, 1944

CORBIS/Bettmann

1851 — Maine enacts America's first statewide alcohol prohibition law. By 1855, 12 more states enact similar bans, though most are repealed before the Civil War.

1880 — The nation's first alcoholism treatment program, using a medicinal form of gold, opens in Dwight, Illinois. Similar programs open in every state, though eventually all either close or end their affiliation with the Keeley method.

1903 — States enact alcohol prohibition laws, affecting a third of the nation. Reformers hope to eliminate social ills, such as poverty and corruption.

1919 — Congress enacts national Prohibition, effective January 16, 1920.

First medical treatment for alcoholism, 1880

Rutgers Center of Alcohol Studies

1920s — Prohibition, losing public support, is enforced unevenly. Between 1921 and 1923, for example, only 27 New Yorkers are convicted of violating the ban.

1933 — National Prohibition is repealed.

1935 — Alcoholics Anonymous, a peer support group, is founded in Akron, Ohio.

1956 — American Medical Association endorses classifying and treating alcoholism as a disease.

1970 — Congress creates the National Institute on Alcohol Abuse and Alcoholism, establishing a public commitment to alcohol–related research.

Alcoholics Anonymous meeting, c. 1950

CORBIS/Bettmann

1970s — Many states lower the legal drinking age, along with the right to vote, to 18 from 21.

1980 — Mothers Against Drunk Driving is founded, expanding to 600 chapters nationwide and encouraging the passage of 2,300 state laws to deter drunk driving.

1984 — To reduce traffic fatalities, the Federal Uniform Drinking Age Act raises the legal drinking age to 21 from 18; by 1988 all states have complied, reducing teen deaths by 1,000 annually.

1985 — The Betty Ford Center for addiction treatment is opened in Rancho Mirage, California, joining the ranks of about 5,000 other facilities nationwide then, and over 10,000 now.

1988 — U.S. Supreme Court refuses to classify alcoholism as a disease, saying that consumption of alcohol is not wholly involuntary.

1989 — Health warning labels are required on all alcohol beverage containers.

1990 — The Americans with Disabilities Act classifies alcoholism as a disability.

1996 — Seagram's airs an ad for liquor on television, violating the industry's 50–year–old voluntary ban on broadcast advertising.

1998 — Los Angeles County prohibits outdoor advertising for alcohol and tobacco within 1,000 feet of residential areas, schools, parks, playgrounds, entertainment centers, and places of worship.

Abuse and Alcoholism, paints a shockingly detailed picture of alcohol abuse and its impact. Some findings:

- Alcohol abuse is involved in 30 percent of suicides, 48 percent of robberies, 50 percent of homicides, 52 percent of rapes and other sexual assaults, 62 percent of assaults, and 68 percent of manslaughter cases.

- A government panel recommended in 1998 that alcohol, which can harm virtually every tissue and organ in the body, be listed officially as a human carcinogen. One in four urban hospital patients – including those with liver disease and breast cancer – is being treated for an ailment linked to alcohol. Alcohol use during pregnancy can cause birth defects, including mental retardation. Among all causes of death, alcohol-related deaths rank third or fourth, from year to year.

> The estimated cost of all alcohol-related problems, $148 billion in 1992, represents $1.09 in societal costs for each drink Americans consume.

- At least 1 percent of all drivers at any time are legally drunk – and on weekend nights that rate rises to 3 percent. Alcohol-related traffic fatalities disproportionately involve the young, annually shortening American lives by nearly half a million years.

- The estimated cost of all alcohol-related problems, $148 billion annually, represents $1.09 in societal costs for each drink Americans consume.

- In 1997, 32 million Americans engaged in binge drinking (having five or more drinks on one occasion), and 11 million were heavy drinkers (bingeing on five or more occasions within the prior month).

- Most young people begin drinking before age 13 and do the heaviest drinking of their lives between the ages of 18 and 21.

Alcohol: A Mixed Blessing

Historians say men, women, and children have been drinking alcohol since about 5000 B.C., when some Neolithic person discovered that all was not lost when fruits and grains spoiled: yeast – a fungus – digested the sugar in plants and excreted alcohol in a process euphemistically called "fermentation." "Alcohol" got its name from the Arabic *al kuhul,* meaning "essence," around 800 A.D., when Arabians discovered how to distill the fermented juices into pure alcohol – a toxic, colorless liquid used as a fuel, solvent, or intoxicating liquor when flavored. Alcohol is considered a drug because it alters moods and is addictive to many, but it is also considered a food because it provides 170 calories of energy per ounce (the fattening equivalent of a dozen oysters). And in the days before refrigeration or water purification, alcoholic drinks offered a measure of safety.

"Booze," derived from a fourteenth-century Dutch word, was considered such a safe and healthful drink that in 1630, when some Puritans set sail for Boston in the ship *Arbella,* they brought three times as much beer as water, as well as 10,000 gallons of wine. According to *Drinking in America,* a history by Mark E. Lender and James K. Martin, everyone in the Colonial family drank beer or fermented ciders with nearly every meal. Strong social norms kept drinking to moderate levels, and drunkenness was shunned as an individual failing or blamed on overly potent liquor. Right up into the early 1800s the military provided sailors and soldiers with daily rations of alcohol, employers offered beer breaks to workers, and "even schoolchildren took their sip of whiskey" in morning and afternoon classes, the authors state. If that seems hard to imagine, consider that, by researchers' best estimates, average per capita consumption of alcohol reached an all-time American record in 1810: 7.1 gallons of pure alcohol, or more than twice the amount consumed in beverages today.

Soon thereafter, the view that alcohol was essential for health began to change, challenged by physicians and public drunkenness. With this change came another: The concept of individual responsibility for drinking lost public support in the face of society's growing inability to cope with alcohol-related crime, injury, and sickness. Personal freedom, as reflected in the names of frontier towns like Delirium Tremens and Gomorrah, had gone too far. Calls for moral stewardship – in the form of alcohol control laws – became common as more Americans came to see alcohol as evil. In 1851 Maine enacted the first state law prohibiting the sale of alcoholic beverages, and 12 other states followed Maine's lead. But the bans, viewed by

Alcohol Abuse: Everyone Pays the Price

Breakdown of costs and percentage of total cost ($148 billion in 1992) stemming from alcohol-related problems, 1998

Alcohol-related illness $67.6 billion

Motor vehicle crashes $13.6 billion

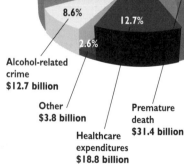

45.7%

9.2%

8.6%

2.6%

12.7%

21.2%

Alcohol-related crime $12.7 billion

Other $3.8 billion

Healthcare expenditures $18.8 billion

Premature death $31.4 billion

Source: *The Economic Costs of Alcohol and Drug Abuse in the United States* —1992. National Institute on Drug Abuse; National Institute on Alcohol Abuse and Alcoholism, 1998

many as an invasion of individual rights, were poorly enforced and were rescinded within a decade. It was the same story with the "Noble Experiment": national Prohibition was enacted in 1919, largely ignored, and rescinded in 1933.

Society's Tool Chest

What is the nation to do? Education, treatment, and law – these are society's primary tools for controlling alcohol abuse, and with today's greater knowledge, each offers more promise than ever before. But in considering the job of reducing alcohol abuse, Americans have some difficult questions to ponder:

Why aren't laws controlling alcohol more effective? Because they are not adequately enforced? Because people don't act rationally when drinking? Because the laws have inadequate public support?

Why don't treatment programs have more impact on the problem? Because many people believe drinking problems are just irresponsible behavior? Because too few people with alcohol problems are in treatment? Because more research is needed to develop better treatments? Because the stigma of alcohol addiction weakens support for expanding treatment and medical training? Or because Americans haven't really gotten the message that abusing alcohol is lethal?

Why aren't education programs having more impact? Because many people do not accept that they drink irresponsibly? Because people need personal health counseling, not general information? Because educational messages lose relevance when role models, sports figures, and actors drink irresponsibly?

Framework for Deliberation

To promote public deliberation about alcohol abuse, this issue book presents three approaches, or choices. These approaches may overlap in certain aspects, but each choice speaks for one distinct set of American priorities and views:

Choice One supporters say most Americans enjoy alcohol and use it responsibly in compliance with laws. Today's problem is that our halfhearted enforcement of alcohol control laws not only makes a mockery of law and moral order, but also encourages illegal alcohol use. People who drink and drive should expect to serve time in jail. To deter abuse, the nation must draw the line on the irresponsible use of alcohol and provide swift, certain, and severe punishment to those who cross that line.

Choice Two supporters say the abuse of alcohol is not a law enforcement problem, but a public health epidemic that the practice of medicine can best cure. Alcoholism is a disease, often inherited, that is shrouded in stigma, confusion, denial, and ignorance. Physicians should screen all patients for alcohol use. In this view, many more programs for prevention, early detection, counseling, and treatment are needed to address the range of alcohol problems leading up to and including addiction.

Choice Three supporters say that progress in enforcing laws or in curbing an epidemic will remain elusive until Americans confront the problems of alcohol abuse – much the way they did with smoking and cancer. Getting drunk should be stigmatized, not laughed at. Using the antismoking campaign as a model, societywide educational efforts would dispel falsehoods and ignorance about alcohol and, at the same time, generate popular social norms and public policies for responsible behavior.

For Further Reading / Alcohol

- Mark Edward Lender and James Kirby Martin, *Drinking in America: A History* (New York: Free Press, 1987).

- U.S. Secretary of Health and Human Services, *Ninth Special Report to the U.S. Congress on Alcohol and Health* (Washington, D.C.: U.S. Department of Health and Human Services, Public Health Service, National Institutes of Health, National Institute on Alcohol Abuse and Alcoholism, June 1997).

- http://www.health.org is the Web site for the National Clearinghouse for Alcohol and Drug Information.

- http://www.niaaa.nih.gov is the Web site for the National Institute on Alcohol Abuse and Alcoholism.

Demand Citizen Responsibility

To deter underage drinking, many police departments participate in a program called Cops in Shops. In it, police work undercover as clerks in liquor stores and arrest minors who attempt to buy alcohol.

Phi Gamma Delta was notorious as the hardest-partying fraternity at the Massachusetts Institute of Technology. The fraternity's parties – including one that evolved into a block party with a rowdy crowd of about 2,000 – regularly spun out of control.

On the average of once every four months between 1992 and 1997, drunken brawls, alcohol-sickened students, or noise complaints brought emergency responses from either the university's police, Boston police, alcohol control officers, or medical technicians, according to a grand jury investigation. So on September 26, 1997, when the fraternity held an "*Animal House* Night," the results were made more tragic by their predictability.

At the party, a dozen freshmen pledges watched the movie *Animal House* while being encouraged to consume a potentially lethal volume of alcohol. Scott Krueger, an 18-year-old freshman with little experience with alcohol, spent the night bingeing on beer, whiskey, and rum. He fell unconscious and asphyxiated on his own vomit, and his lungs and heart stopped working. Emergency medical technicians revived him, but he was pronounced dead in the morning as his parents and sister gathered around his hospital bed.

The death stunned Boston, but what could be done to prevent underage drinking? Area colleges have since imposed stricter rules and punishments for illegal drinking, and a new police crackdown on illegal alcohol purchases is making Boston-area teenagers think twice about trying to buy liquor. Police, with the cooperation of liquor store owners, pose as liquor store clerks and prevent teenagers from buying alcohol with phony IDs. Youthful offenders are arrested, are fined up to $300, and lose their driver's license for 90 days. "The point is not to make wholesale arrests of college students, but the message is, if you procure alcohol with a fake ID in Boston, you may be arrested," Boston police captain Charles J. Cellucci told the *Boston Globe* in September 1998 after one sting operation netted 12 minors with false IDs and 1 adult who was buying for minors. The Boston-area program is modeled after a national one called Cops in Shops, which was developed with research assistance from the alcohol industry. Alcohol beverage control agents in 15 participating states endorsed the program, saying that it increases public awareness about underage drinking and deters purchases by minors, according to a survey by the National Association of Governors' Highway Safety Representatives.

A Right to Drink (Responsibly)

Phi Gamma Delta's ability to flout alcohol laws for years is just one illustration of how lax society has become in enforcing alcohol control laws. Similarly, the Cops in Shops program is just one example of how society can enforce societal norms for drinking. These norms are written into our laws, but they are meaningless if police do not enforce them with the kind of rapidity, certainty, and severity that is known to encourage compliance.

It's time, say supporters, for the nation to seriously enforce alcohol control laws. Choice One acknowledges that most Americans enjoy alcohol and use it responsibly, knowing its potential dangers. Supporters add that an adult's right to drink alcohol is really a right to drink responsibly. Drinking irresponsibly, such as when a person intends to drive, is destructive behavior that society must deter with strict enforcement of alcohol laws. Uneven enforcement of these laws got us where we are today, in this view.

Choice One supporters also say that some new laws are still needed to deter specific problems, such as underage drinking. And because alcohol problems are so huge – exceeding those associated with all illegal drugs combined – Choice One calls for the nation to reorder its priorities and dedicate a larger share of public resources to refining and enforcing laws to control alcohol abuse.

Taking Control

The main obstacle to reducing alcohol abuse, in this view, is a wavering public commitment to enforce laws. Why? The answer goes to the heart of the nation's difficulties with alcohol abuse, say Choice One supporters. They cite two major reasons for public ambivalence: First, America still shares a worldwide tradition of accepting alcohol-related problems as an inevitable, immutable part of life. Second, there is a modern reluctance to hold anyone fully responsible for unintentional behavior that can

What Can Be Done ?

Supporters of Choice One generally favor the following measures:

- Strengthen alcohol control laws to deter irresponsible drinking behavior. Maximize the deterrent value of laws by making sure they provide for rapid, certain, and severe punishment to offenders. Substantially increase enforcement of existing alcohol control laws.

- Give a much higher priority to enforcing alcohol control laws, as alcohol problems are more socially damaging than those associated with all illegal drugs combined.

- Close outlets that negligently sell alcohol to minors. Punish minors who try to buy alcohol, and punish adults who sell alcohol to minors.

- Tighten community zoning laws to limit the number of alcohol retailers, as higher crime rates are associated with higher numbers of alcohol outlets.

- Reduce drunk driving with stricter laws and enforcement. For example:

  - Sharply reduce the legal threshold for drunken driving, reflecting research findings that one drink can turn a driver into a highway hazard.

  - Arrest minors who have drunk any alcohol before driving and suspend their driver's licenses for a year.

  - Require offenders to display a "Convicted for Driving Under the Influence of Alcohol" bumper sticker, which permits police in some states to make random sobriety checks.

  - Substantially increase penalties for repeat offenders. Keep them off the road by any means necessary, including driver's license revocation, vehicle and license plate seizure, and substantial jail sentences.

be blamed on the effects of alcohol. Society cuts even more slack for people who chronically abuse alcohol, based on the theory that alcoholism is a disease and drunken behavior is merely an involuntary symptom.

Choice One supporters call for Americans to reconsider these views. First, Americans should recognize that alcohol-related tragedies like traffic fatalities are not accidents, but the predictable results of irresponsible drinking. Second, alcoholism is universally defined as an addiction to the drug alcohol. Some experts go further, asserting that this addiction is a "disease" because the vulnerability to alcohol seems to have an inherited, biological basis. This is a popular idea, an easy way to explain why so many good people have bad drinking habits. Yet unlike diabetes, cancer, or heart disease, alcoholism involves a decision to drink. The U.S. Supreme Court, no less, refuses to classify alcoholism as a disease, saying in a 1988 decision that "consumption of alcohol, even among those who consider alcoholism a disease, is not regarded as wholly involuntary."

In any event, Choice One says that portraying alcoholism as a disease is counterproductive: in providing a medical alibi for irresponsible drinking behavior, society provides a legitimate excuse for its continuation – to everyone's detriment.

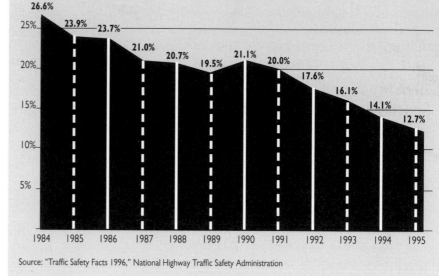

Laws Save Lives

Percentage of teenage drivers killed in motor vehicle crashes while under the influence of alcohol, 1995 (Note: In 1984 Congress raised the legal drinking age to 21 from 18.)

- 1984: 26.6%
- 1985: 23.9%
- 1986: 23.7%
- 1987: 21.0%
- 1988: 20.7%
- 1989: 19.5%
- 1990: 21.1%
- 1991: 20.0%
- 1992: 17.6%
- 1993: 16.1%
- 1994: 14.1%
- 1995: 12.7%

Source: "Traffic Safety Facts 1996," National Highway Traffic Safety Administration

Realistic Laws and Enforcement

Scientists are making great strides in understanding and deterring irresponsible drinking, but Choice One supporters assert that the nation has been slow to apply this research widely. Consider one of the most serious problems, driving while under the influence of alcohol.

Better laws are needed. Alcohol, starting with the smallest amounts that can be measured, impairs the brain's ability to receive, interpret, and process information – with the result that drivers who have had any alcohol are measurably less attentive, less observant, less responsive, and less skilled in steering and braking. Numerous experiments, some decades old, have established that driving ability begins to be impaired after a single drink, but laws do not reflect this reality. Instead, most legal limits for drinking send an incorrect signal that people can still drive safely after two or more drinks. In 1989 C. Everett Koop, the U.S. surgeon general, called for states to correct this message by slashing the legal threshold for intoxication and impairment to 0.04 percent blood alcohol concentration (from 0.1 percent); since then, however, only 17 states have overcome the alcohol industry's fierce opposition to stricter limits on drinking before driving, and even in those cases the reduction was negligible (to 0.08 percent).

Better enforcement is needed. Laws are effective when people know the rules and see that violators receive rapid and certain punishment. Sobriety checkpoints, for example, are a successful way to enforce drunk driving laws – yet checkpoints are rarely used.

The effectiveness of sobriety checkpoints has been demonstrated in the

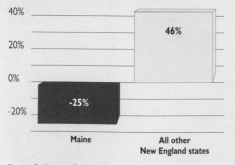

Stronger Laws, Safer Roads

Percentage change in traffic fatalities between 1988 and 1994, associated with drunk driving in Maine and all other New England states, 1996
(Note: In 1988 Maine lowered the legal threshold for driving under the influence to 0.08% from 0.10% blood alcohol concentration; other New England states did not lower the threshold.)

- Maine: -25%
- All other New England states: 46%

Source: R. Hingson, T. Heeren, M. Winter, "Lowering State Legal Blood Alcohol Limits to 0.08%: The Effect on Fatal Motor Vehicle Crashes," *American Journal of Public Health* 86(9): 1,297–1,299, 1996

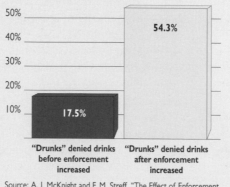

When Police Patrol Bars, Fewer Drunks Get Served

Percentage of study participants who, while acting drunk, were denied additional alcoholic drinks at bars and restaurants, before and after police in Washtenaw County, Michigan, increased law enforcement, 1994

- "Drunks" denied drinks before enforcement increased: 17.5%
- "Drunks" denied drinks after enforcement increased: 54.3%

Source: A. J. McKnight and F. M. Streff, "The Effect of Enforcement Upon Service of Alcohol to Intoxicated Patrons of Bars and Restaurants," *Accident Analysis and Prevention* 26(1):79–88, 1994

small town of Rumford, Maine. There, police ask the local media to publicize plans about when and where police will stop every vehicle for a quick driver check. At the checkpoint, one police officer politely asks if the driver has been drinking, while others scan the vehicle for violations such as a missing license plate. If the driver admits to drinking or shows signs of intoxication, or if there is a vehicle violation, police have authority to administer dexterity and vision tests for sobriety, followed up when necessary by an arrest and formal breath test at the police station.

Punishment is swift and certain. If a driver refuses to take the breath test or fails it, his or her license is immediately suspended, pending a court appearance. Penalties – including fines, jail sentences, license revocation, and vehicle confiscation – increase with each offense to deter repeat offenders. Also, if drivers under 21 fail the sobriety test by exhibiting any measurable alcohol level, they automatically lose their driver's licenses for one year. National research indicates that the immediate loss of a driver's license is very effective in reducing subsequent drinking and driving violations.

The sobriety checkpoint program in Rumford, supported by a yearly $10,000 state grant, is paying big dividends, said Sergeant George Cayer, who is in charge of the program. "I have seen our 'operating under the influence' arrest rate drop from over 125 arrests a year to 82 arrests last year," he confirmed. Alcohol-related fatal crashes, once occurring every few months, have now become a rarity. "Rumford citizens are well aware that operating under the influence is not tolerated in our community and if they choose to drink and drive, they will most likely get caught."

> **"I have seen our 'operating under the influence' arrest rate drop from over 125 arrests a year to 82 arrests last year."**

Well-publicized sobriety checkpoints in Rumford, Maine, have greatly reduced the number of people arrested for drinking and driving, say police.

Closing bars that serve drunk or underage customers is one way to hold the alcohol industry accountable.

In Support

✓ Americans have a right to drink alcohol, but no right to drink so much that they harm others. Strict law enforcement deters irresponsible drinking.

✓ There is no mystery about the ill effects of alcohol, and there should be no excuse for intoxicated misbehavior. Alcohol-related motor vehicle crashes, for example, are not accidents – they are predictable crimes associated with deliberately misusing alcohol and then driving.

✓ Americans may want to excuse bad behavior by good people who become incapacitated by alcohol, but this only encourages irresponsible drinking.

✓ The nation's laws convey social norms for the responsible use of alcohol. But the nation's failure to adequately enforce these laws makes a mockery of them. As it is, most Americans do their heaviest drinking illegally – under age 21.

✓ Laws should be amended to reflect research about risks. For example, current laws permit driving with a blood alcohol concentration of just under 0.08 percent in any state. However, recent government-sponsored research has shown that a driver with that level of blood alcohol concentration is 11 times more likely to be involved in a crash than someone who has not drunk any alcohol. Based on this research, states should lower the legally accepted threshold for drunk driving.

✓ Strict laws and enforcement successfully deter alcohol misuse. In Maryland, for example, a 1992 study reported a 50 percent decline in motor vehicle fatalities involving minors after passage of a law authorizing police to revoke the licenses of minors who drive after having a single drink.

Niculae Asciu

In Opposition

✗ This choice calls for more of the same unsatisfactory approach the nation has pursued for years. For example, drunk driving persists as a major problem even though police arrest two million intoxicated drivers a year and even though states have enacted 2,300 laws against drunk driving since 1980, according to government statistics. We need new ideas.

✗ In calling for jailing more drunken drivers, this choice would require more prisons to be built. It would also clog prisons with people who need treatment more than they need punishment.

✗ Even though this choice calls for deterring only irresponsible drinking behavior, it really takes away the right to drink responsibly. For example, this choice would forbid almost any drinking before driving, while the record indicates that drunk driving accidents are caused primarily by very inebriated drivers.

✗ Among advocates of this approach, there are those who say it doesn't go far enough: alcohol use should be banned entirely, they say.

✗ The ends do not justify the means, and this choice's goal of reducing alcohol abuse does not justify violations of Americans' constitutional rights. Undercover police should not be allowed to entrap minors in crime; and courts, not police, should decide whether a driver's license is suspended.

✗ Until there is more widespread agreement about the appropriate use of alcohol, there will never be enough public support for stricter laws or enforcement.

✗ This choice focuses on enforcement and deterrence, but it is less expensive and less harmful in the long run to focus on prevention and treatment.

For Further Reading / Demand Citizen Responsibility

■ Stanton Peele, *The Diseasing of America* (New York: Lexington Books, an imprint of the Free Press, 1995).

■ Bobby Little and Mike Bishop, "Minor Drinkers/Major Consequences: Enforcement Strategies for Underage Alcoholic Beverage Law Violators," *FBI Law Enforcement Bulletin*, vol. 67, June 1, 1998.

■ http://www.madd.org is the Web site for MADD, Mothers Against Drunk Driving, a national organization that has raised awareness about the dangers of driving under the influence and lobbied successfully for stricter laws around alcohol and driving.

Treat the Public Health Epidemic

Lara Jo Regan/Gamma Liaison

Former First Lady Betty Ford, far right, greets new patients at the alcohol and drug treatment center named after her in Rancho Mirage, California.

Betty Ford, one of America's most popular First Ladies, is best known for her courage in breaking the nation's deadly silence about two diseases, breast cancer in 1974 and alcoholism in 1978. In both instances she decided to share her most intimate feelings, because along her path of treatment and recovery she was forced to overcome her own ignorance, fear, and prejudice about these ailments – the same public attitudes, she realized, that were enabling these diseases to spread with epidemic speed.

So she spoke about what it means for a woman to lose a breast and the need for regular check-ups. And she spoke about what it means to suffer from alcohol addiction, which because of its blinding stigma goes unrecognized and untreated as a disease, especially among women. "Women couldn't be alcoholic, and certainly the wife of a former president couldn't be involved in anything so disgusting," she wrote wryly in her 1987 memoir, *Betty, A Glad Awakening*.

Family, friends, physicians, and even Mrs. Ford failed to recognize that she was ill, addicted to alcohol and, later on, prescription drugs for neck pain. "Drinking was a way we relaxed, a way we celebrated, and it was good until it went bad," she wrote. "If you're not an alcoholic, it doesn't have to go bad, but I'm an alcoholic. I just didn't know it for 30 years." By 1978, during her second retirement year in California, the disease had become obvious, turning her into a "zombie" who spent most of her day in a bathrobe. Pressured by her family, she entered a detoxification treatment program and began the

Supporters of Choice Two generally favor the following measures:

- Organize a national, comprehensive healthcare response to the epidemic of alcohol abuse.

- Substantially increase public funding of research, prevention, and treatment programs. Anyone who wants treatment should be able to receive it.

- Provide a fast track process for approving new drugs to treat alcohol problems.

- Set the record straight. Leaders in the medical community should take steps to dispel false stereotypes held by healthcare professionals.

- Greatly expand instruction about alcohol abuse in medical and nursing schools.

- Make it standard medical practice to screen all patients, young and old, for alcohol use and abuse, much as blood pressure and cholesterol tests are given today. Provide patients with medical information and referrals for treatment.

- Counter binge drinking in high school and college with comprehensive medical screening and counseling programs.

- Encourage more employers to meet employees' needs for counseling and treatment through employee assistance programs.

- Provide alcohol treatment, instead of punishment, to people who break alcohol laws but do not harm others. Provide prison inmates with alcohol and drug treatment before releasing them.

- Require health insurers, including government and student insurers, to cover medical costs of treating alcoholism and alcohol abuse, much as insurers cover other health problems.

long, hard journey toward recovery. En route, the journey became a mission, to help others by dispelling the stigma of alcoholism, which serves only to delay diagnosis and treatment, to prolong family suffering. In 1984 that mission took the form of the Betty Ford Center, a residential treatment program she helped establish in Rancho Mirage, California.

Looking back, an 80-year-old Mrs. Ford told *Dateline NBC* in 1998 that, all things considered, it was "tougher" dealing with alcoholism than with cancer. Choice Two supporters say this shouldn't be so.

It's a Silent Epidemic

The American Medical Association recognized alcoholism as a disease in 1955. But stigma, confusion, denial, and even apathy still surround the problem of alcoholism and alcohol abuse, enabling it to become the nation's most severe public health epidemic, say Choice One supporters. The epidemic has many faces, including teenagers drinking to get drunk, inebriated adults becoming violent, and hospital patients dying from alcohol-related diseases. At its center, it is an eerily silent epidemic. The sick suffer in private, as people with an alcohol problem are the very last to admit it, even to themselves. Compounding that denial, society notices alcohol problems only when they become shocking, and even then focuses mostly on the behavior, not the disease.

Unfortunately, most frightening diseases go through these tragic phases of confusion. Before tuberculosis was well understood, for example, physicians widely debated whether TB was a disease or a "behavioral problem," as symptoms often included erratic behavior, aggression, blackouts, and irritability. It seems to be human nature, perhaps a survival instinct, to initially react to life-threatening plagues like cancer or AIDS by blaming the victims for irresponsible behavior and shunning them to isolate the problem.

The prior choice takes this approach, seeing alcohol problems as irresponsible behavior to be corrected and, if necessary, isolated in prison cells. But laws and jails have never resolved a public health epidemic, say Choice Two supporters. In this view, our legal system perpetuates the epidemic in two ways: in some cases, by substituting punishment for minor offenses where treatment is more appropriate; in other cases, where punishment is appropriate, by failing to provide prison inmates with treatment for alcohol and drug addiction before returning them to the streets.

The resolution for this epidemic rests on the shoulders of medical science, say Choice Two supporters. They call for a major public health initiative to increase scientific, professional, and patient understanding of alcohol-related health problems, treatment, and prevention. Among other things, substantially more research is needed to understand and treat the disease, including the development of additional medicines. Medical schools, which currently devote less than 1 percent of their curriculum to alcohol and drug addiction, should teach extensive courses in these areas. Physicians should routinely screen all patients – young and old – for alcohol use, providing appropriate warnings and making referrals for treatment. Health insurers, including government and student health insurers, must stop discriminating against

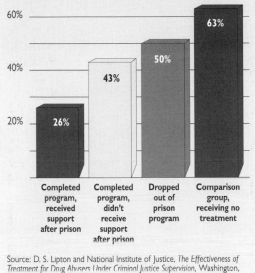

Treating Inmates Reduces Crime

Percentage of inmates reincarcerated for crimes a year after parole, according to their level of participation in Amity Righturn, a prison-based alcohol and drug addiction treatment program, 1995

Completed program, received support after prison	Completed program, didn't receive support after prison	Dropped out of prison program	Comparison group, receiving no treatment
26%	43%	50%	63%

Source: D. S. Lipton and National Institute of Justice, *The Effectiveness of Treatment for Drug Abusers Under Criminal Justice Supervision*, Washington, D.C.: Department of Justice, Office of Justice Programs, National Institute of Justice, 1995

Medical associations say physicians could go a long way toward preventing and reducing alcohol abuse by screening patients of all ages and offering them counseling and referrals for alcohol misuse.

porters. But as research accumulates and more leaders speak out, they see momentum building behind the need to address the public health epidemic. In her periodic reports to Congress, for example, Donna E. Shalala, U.S. secretary of health and human services, has been blunt about the epidemic, which she says affects one in four Americans and disables one in ten adults. The answer, she emphasized in 1993, is prevention and treatment: "We can be confident that, like other diseases that once caused widespread pain and suffering, alcohol abuse and alcoholism will one day yield to the preventive and treatment measures derived from today's scientific discoveries."

What's missing, say Choice Two supporters, is a national sense of urgency and a financial commitment commensurate with the gravity of the epidemic of alcohol problems. Consider a symbolic illustration of this imbalance: For fiscal year 1999, the National Institute on Alcohol Abuse and Alcoholism, the nation's leading agency on alcoholism, has a budget of only $260 million at a time when the epidemic is responsible for one in five deaths – annually killing

alcoholism and cover the medical costs as they do other health problems.

Many more programs for prevention, early detection, and treatment are needed to address the range of alcohol problems leading up to and including addiction. New programs are especially needed on college campuses. One pioneer, the University of Maryland, has set up a Web site on the Internet so that its students can confidentially assess their own risks for problems with alcohol or other drugs and then obtain referrals for counseling and treatment.

A Time to Act

The nation made little progress with diseases like TB or AIDS until society stopped paying lip service to the ailments and started committing major resources to medical research, prevention, and treatment. Alcoholism and alcohol abuse are still in the lip service stage, say Choice Two sup-

Given the prevalence and severity of alcohol problems in America, far too little research is being conducted, say Choice Two supporters.

Most Treatment Works

Percentage of patients in an alcohol treatment program who remained abstinent 12 months after treatment, 1995

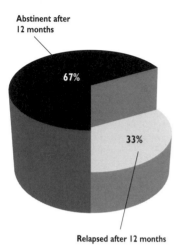

Abstinent after 12 months

67%

33%

Relapsed after 12 months

Source: Betty Ford Center, 1995

100,000, mostly people in their prime. Patients stricken with alcohol-related diseases fill one in four urban hospital beds.

Yet evidence of society's failure to take this epidemic seriously is also detailed in the secretary's reports. For instance, a 1991 hospital study indicates that physicians overlook alcohol in diagnosing two out of three patients with alcohol-related health problems. Researchers draw the obvious conclusion: Medical care and prevention strategies would be greatly improved if physicians routinely screened their patients for evidence of alcohol use and abuse. Other studies indicate that physicians encourage fewer than one in five Americans with an alcohol problem to seek treatment. It's shocking, but less so when one considers that medical school students receive hardly any training in diagnosing and treating alcohol-related problems. Only 4 in 121 medical schools, for example, require a separate course on alcohol and drug abuse, according to the Institute of Medicine. Medical journals such as *Lancet* also report that physicians commonly hold false stereotypes of alcohol problems and treatment.

Manageable Health Problems

The Betty Ford Center is one of the nation's best regarded residential treatment facilities, offering a three-to-four-week program for 80 patients from all walks of life. After going through detoxification treatment, patients participate in an individualized recovery program developed by a team that includes a physician, nurse, psychologist, dietitian, pastoral care counselor, and family counselor. In the center's follow-up studies of patients a year after treatment, it was revealed that more than 60 percent remained abstinent from alcohol and other drugs. "Our goal with our patients is to help equip them with powerful tools to live with their condition," the center's brochure states. "But make no mistake. Diseases like alcoholism aren't conquered…but can be rendered manageable."

Medical science has a long way to go, even though alcoholism has for years been recognized as a disease of the brain and liver. It is not well understood how alcohol works in the body, but its simple molecular structure permits it to pass right through the protective cell membranes of every tissue and organ, including the brain. Within minutes of being consumed, then, alcohol widely disrupts cellular activity, acting first as a stimulant and then, in higher concentrations, as a sedative on emotions, thought, speech, and coordination.

Alcoholism, like diabetes, is defined as a chronic, relapsing, incurable disease that requires lifelong management. The term *alcohol abuse* covers both chronic and isolated instances of misuse. Like many diseases, alcoholism tends to run in families, and in hopes of developing early detection and prevention programs, scientists are trying to isolate the specific genes that predispose millions to alcohol abuse. With such knowledge, physicians would be able to screen patients and counsel those most susceptible to alcoholism and alcohol abuse. But millions of people without alcoholism in their family tree also develop alcohol problems, leaving a mystery for scientists to explain.

Choice Two supporters assert that a nationwide application of existing knowledge about prevention and treatment could contain the epidemic. They say the nation does not have to wait until all the answers are in and all the skeptics are satisfied.

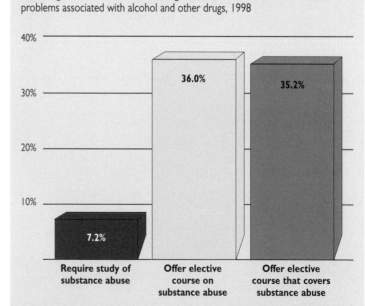

Medical Schools Provide Little Training

Percentage of medical schools offering instruction in the treatment of health problems associated with alcohol and other drugs, 1998

Require study of substance abuse	Offer elective course on substance abuse	Offer elective course that covers substance abuse
7.2%	36.0%	35.2%

Source: Barbara Barzansky, Harry S. Jonas, Sylvia I. Etzel, "Education Programs in U.S. Medical Schools, 1997–98," *Journal of the American Medical Association* 280: 803–808, 1997–98 Liaison Committee on Medical Education Annual Medical Schools Questionnaire, American Medical Association, 1998

In Support

✓ Alcoholism and alcohol abuse account for more economic and social damage than any other public health problem, yet the epidemic rages on, largely ignored and untreated.

✓ By any measure, the nation is not committing adequate resources to medical research, treatment, and prevention of alcohol problems, which, the government says, affect one in four Americans, disable one in ten adults, and cause or contribute to one in five deaths.

✓ The American Medical Association recognized alcoholism as a disease in 1955, yet, paradoxically, medical schools teach few courses about the disease and most physicians fail to diagnose or treat alcohol problems.

✓ Alcohol abuse is a health problem, one that can destroy the mind and body. When physicians tell that to the young, they listen. They rebel against rules.

✓ This is what the U.S. Department of Health and Human Services says: Treatment for alcohol problems is effective, and recovery is possible for many.

✓ It is less costly, and better for society in the long run, to treat people for problems with alcohol and other drugs than it is to jail them for minor, nonviolent offenses related to their alcohol and drug use.

✓ One in every 141 adults in America is behind bars for alcohol- and drug-related crimes, at a cost to taxpayers of $30 billion in 1996. Because of the extreme shortage of treatment programs in prison, these offenders return to the community the way they left, suffering from addictions and heading for trouble.

In Opposition

✗ Paradoxically, this choice calls for a major medical response at a time when many physicians consider alcoholism to be a bad habit, not a disease, and when medical schools devote little attention to it as a health problem.

✗ Portraying alcoholics as hapless victims of disease ignores their decision to drink and undermines their power to control their drinking. Society shouldn't give irresponsible drinkers a medical excuse to avoid responsibility and accountability.

✗ This choice calls for a massive medical response to the problems of alcohol at a time when the role of medicine in this area is most uncertain. A pair of studies published in the July 1996 *American Journal of Public Health,* for example, found that three out of four people who had recovered from alcohol did so without any outside help or treatment.

✗ Why spend more public funds on treatment when one of the best is free? A $29 million study of verbal treatment programs, sponsored by the National Institute on Alcohol Abuse and Alcoholism, reported in 1997 that peer support groups, such as Alcoholics Anonymous, are as effective as two other kinds of costly counseling programs.

✗ This choice focuses on serious alcohol problems, but what about social drinkers who engage in irresponsible behavior like drinking and driving? Only laws and their enforcement can deter that behavior.

✗ Unfortunately, no treatment program can prevent relapses into irresponsible drinking, but laws can deter irresponsible behavior.

For Further Reading / Treat the Public Health Epidemic

■ Don R. Mowery, "Long-Term Rehabilitation Is Costly, but It Works," *San Diego Union-Tribune,* July 4, 1997.

■ Mike Mitka, "'Teachable Moments' Provide a Means for Physicians to Lower Alcohol Abuse," *JAMA Medical News & Perspectives,* vol. 279, June 10, 1998.

■ http://www.asam.org is the Web site for the American Society of Addiction Medicine.

Niculae Asciu

Educate for Societal Change

CORBIS/Steve Chenn

Portrayal of alcohol abuse on TV should be sobering, not entertaining.

Actor Scott Wolf, who made it onto *People* magazine's 1998 "50 Most Beautiful People" list, plays Bailey Salinger, a college freshman, on *A Party of Five,* a popular television series for teenagers and young adults on the Fox Broadcasting Company network. After establishing Salinger as the show's most likable person, the dramatic series darkened his characterization with a drinking problem.

In one episode his drinking spoiled his brother's birthday party. In another his drinking caused a car crash that injured his girlfriend. "In the long run, Bailey is going to deal with his problem, and people are going to be there for him," Christopher Keyser, one of the show's producers, told the *Buffalo News* in 1997. "But it's not going to be easy. They're not going to all want to be there. And there are going to be other personal conflicts that stand in their way, and it won't be easy for Bailey to get to the point where he says, 'I can be okay with myself and stop drinking.' There's no question that the point of view of the show is, 'Don't drink.'" The newspaper's TV critic, Alan Pergament, gave the drunk driving episode a four-star rating out of five, writing, "It is lump-in-your-throat stuff. Don't miss it."

The episodes on drinking won the show a public service award in 1998 for accurately portraying problems associated with alcohol. The PRISM Awards program, launched in 1997, stands in recognition of the social problems caused when the entertainment media glamorizes unhealthy activities like smoking and drinking. The sponsors of PRISM include a philanthropic foundation, an entertainment industry association, and a government agency – the National Institute on Drug Abuse, which sponsors most research on the health aspects of drug addiction. The awards program recognizes the huge role the entertainment media has in shaping public opinion, said an institute spokesman. "What we are trying to do is co-opt the entertainment industry to educate people about the nature of drug abuse and addiction in an accurate way," he said. "And we're getting more and more inquiries from film companies, networks, and broadcast companies asking us, 'Is this an accurate portrayal?'"

Needed: New Social Norms

Choice Three supporters praise shows like *A Party of Five* for countering the pervasive message in popular culture that excessive drinking is cool, sexy, and smart. That accuracy wins awards, however, says a lot about the inaccurate way alcohol is presented in music, film, and TV – not to mention advertising that links drinking with sex, sports, and success. Society can't afford to be misled this way when alcohol abuse is linked to every imaginable human tragedy, including birth defects like mental retardation, most incidents of spousal abuse, one in three drownings, half of the adult fatalities in house fires – and even one of the nation's worst environmental disasters. In 1989 the *Exxon Valdez,* a supertanker skippered by a man who had been drinking, spilled 11 million gallons of crude oil into Alaska's Prince William Sound.

Supporters say that it is one thing for dangerous products like alcohol and tobacco to be legally available for adult enjoyment, but it is wrong for these industries to woo young consumers and promote excessive use. The key to reducing abuse, say supporters, is making sure that Americans, especially the young, have a very clear grasp of alcohol's ill effects on health, family, and work. Public ignorance about alcohol's effects is widespread, as just a few studies suggest:

■ One in four women said they *have not heard* of fetal alcohol syndrome and do not know that any alcohol consumption at all during pregnancy can cause birth defects, according to a 1990 government sponsored study.

■ Most Americans do not know that legal levels of drinking can substantially impair driving skills, government research indicates.

■ Most young men aged 18 to 24 cannot define "moderate drinking" – the two-drink-a-day level that nutritional guidelines say is safe and healthy for men – according to a 1997 survey by EDK Associates. Among those men who don't know, 76 percent report binge drinking – five or more drinks in a day.

Education dispels ignorance and motivates action. After all, it was public education – in schools, public awareness campaigns, government warnings, and even the news and entertainment media – that changed social norms for smoking. Adults stopped smoking in most public places and smoked less in private; many teenagers also saw it was no longer cool to smoke. By popular demand some social norms, like not smoking

What Can Be Done ?

Supporters of Choice Three generally favor the following measures:

■ Reduce alcohol abuse with the same kind of educational approach that is working successfully with smoking.

■ Expand school programs on the drug alcohol, modeled on successful ones that help young people realize it isn't cool, smart, or sexy to smoke.

■ Decrease alcohol consumption, especially among underage drinkers, by increasing alcohol taxes to support public education campaigns.

■ Use massive public awareness campaigns to overcome the nation's lack of knowledge about such things as safe and healthy drinking levels. Role models, especially parents, can show how they limit alcohol consumption to a healthy amount.

■ Encourage new social norms for safe drinking, much as citizens did to curb smoking. For example, a new social norm that might grow out of an educational program could be "No drinking before driving." Another could be "Getting drunk isn't funny, it's sickening."

■ Insist that the alcohol industry reinstitute its former voluntary ban on liquor advertising on radio and television. Seek a similar ban on wine and beer advertising.

■ Clarify and rotate the warning labels on alcohol products – and advertising – so that they are more comprehensive and more noticeable.

■ Use boycotts and protests to stop advertising and marketing campaigns that promote excessive drinking and appeal to people under 21.

■ Reject alcohol industry sponsorship and promotions for alcohol in sports arenas and civic celebrations.

■ Insist that the entertainment media stop glamorizing alcohol consumption and, instead, portray its costs and benefits accurately.

in public, evolved into public policies – which citizens themselves play an active role in enforcing, as any smoker in an airplane or restaurant quickly discovers. According to the U.S. Department of Health and Human Services, "The major factor that resulted in dramatic decreases in the number and pattern of persons who use tobacco products was primarily related to changes in social norms."

Choice Three's educational approach to alcohol would also encourage an informed citizenry to act on their own conclusions, *creating new social norms for drinking, much as they did for smoking*. New social norms, then, would guide individual decisions about drinking and public views about advertising, marketing, and the depiction of alcohol in popular culture. These norms would essentially specify what

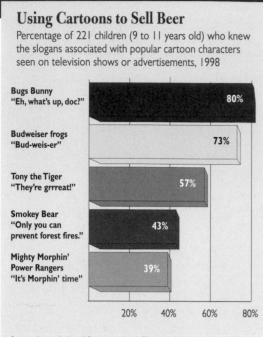

Using Cartoons to Sell Beer

Percentage of 221 children (9 to 11 years old) who knew the slogans associated with popular cartoon characters seen on television shows or advertisements, 1998

Bugs Bunny
"Eh, what's up, doc?" — 80%

Budweiser frogs
"Bud-weis-er" — 73%

Tony the Tiger
"They're grrreat!" — 57%

Smokey Bear
"Only you can prevent forest fires." — 43%

Mighty Morphin'
Power Rangers
"It's Morphin' time" — 39%

20% 40% 60% 80%

Source: Laurie Leiber, "Commercial and Character Slogan Recall by Children Aged 9 to 11 years: Budweiser Frogs versus Bugs Bunny," Center on Alcohol Advertising, 1998

complies, or doesn't comply, with the one long-held public view: Only adults should drink alcohol, and they should drink in a safe and responsible manner. As with the social revolution in smoking, Americans would exert their will through community protests, boycotts, and demands for changes in public policy. A Catholic church on Chicago's South Side, for example, is campaigning against the proliferation of alcohol and tobacco billboards in minority communities, and these bans on billboards have been passed in Baltimore.

If the nation's experience with tobacco is a guide, say Choice Three supporters, change in alcohol consumption would follow education but would not follow isolated efforts to increase law enforcement or treatment programs, as the prior choices advocate. From the Choice Three perspective, then: Choice One would impose laws that, without widespread public support, would work no better than existing alcohol control laws that are widely flouted; Choice Two imposes a medical solution, but one that lacks solid support in the medical community and casts citizens in the narrow role of patient.

Popular Culture as Public Education

Education about alcohol must start with its accurate depiction in popular culture, say Choice Three supporters. The potential influence of television advertising and programming on behavior is enormous, say researchers, especially for children and teenagers, who spend more time in front of the TV than they spend in school. There are good shows, such as the award-winning *A Party of Five*, but overall the entertainment media glamorizes and promotes drinking. Some examples:

■ Nearly all of the most popular films from 1985 to 1995 contained positive – but few or no negative – references to smoking and drinking, accord-

Damian Dovarganes/AP/Wide World Photos

Whether it's St. Patrick's Day or Cinco de Mayo, a Mexican American folk festival, parades have become excuses for heavy drinking – and saturation advertising of alcoholic beverages. In 1998, civic leaders in California reemphasized the ethnic spirit of Cinco de Mayo – and campaigned against alcohol industry efforts to promote the folk festival as a beer festival.

ing to a 1998 study at the Allegheny University of Health Sciences.

■ Ninety-one percent of boys and 70 percent of girls aged 9 to 11 can correctly recall Budweiser's cartoon frogs and their song ("Bud-weis-er"), a higher rate of recall than for four other popular cartoon characters and their slogans, including the Mighty Morphin' Power Rangers ("It's Morphin' time"), according to a 1997 study by the Center on Alcohol Advertising.

■ Young people who watch a lot of TV, especially music videos, are more likely to become teenage drinkers, according to a 1998 Stanford University study that tracked teenagers over 18 months. TV characters who drink, the study found, are usually "attractive, successful, and influential, and they drink alcoholic beverages in a positive social context, often associated with sexually suggestive content, recreation, or motor vehicle use; alcohol is rarely portrayed in an unattractive way or shown to have negative consequences."

Asked to comment on the Stanford study's findings, an 11-year-old girl told CNN News she was not surprised. About drinking alcohol, she said: "It's like it's really cool. And I want to do it, too, so I can be cool."

Clearly, says Choice Three, the nation has to come to grips with a popular culture that promotes alcohol and bombards children with dangerous messages. According to government-sponsored research, young people who take up drinking before age 15 tend to develop more alcohol problems – and are *four times* more likely to develop an addiction to alcohol – than their peers who wait until age 21 to drink. Yet a 1994 study at Michigan State University reported that a majority of American youth begin drinking before their thirteenth birthday, that three in ten teenagers have a drinking problem, and that most Americans will do their heaviest drinking before turning 21.

School Programs Reduce Substance Use

Percentage reduction in drinking, smoking, marijuana use, and multiple drug use by students six years after completing a school program on substance abuse that teaches decision-making skills and promotes self-esteem, 1995
(Note: In the first two bars, percentages reflect a range in reduction of substance use.)

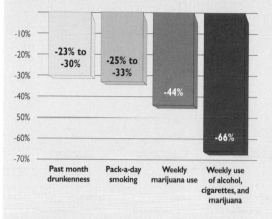

Past month drunkenness	**Pack-a-day smoking**	**Weekly marijuana use**	**Weekly use of alcohol, cigarettes, and marijuana**
-23% to -30%	-25% to -33%	-44%	-66%

Source: G. J. Botvin, E. Baker, L. Dusenbury, E. Botvin, T. Diaz, "Long-Term Follow-up Results of a Randomized Drug Abuse Prevention Trial in a White Middle-Class Population," *Journal of the American Medical Association* 273(14): 1,106–12, 1995

Education Needed About Alcohol-Related Birth Defects

Percentage of a nationally representative sample of women and men who said they had heard of fetal alcohol syndrome – birth defects, including mental retardation, caused by drinking during pregnancy – and the percentage of respondents who accurately described the syndrome as alcohol-induced birth defects, 1990

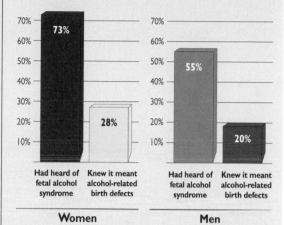

Women		**Men**	
Had heard of fetal alcohol syndrome	Knew it meant alcohol-related birth defects	Had heard of fetal alcohol syndrome	Knew it meant alcohol-related birth defects
73%	28%	55%	20%

Source: Mary C. Dufur, Gerald D. Williams, Karen E. Campbell, and Sherrie S. Aitken, "Knowledge of FAS and the Risks of Heavy Drinking During Pregnancy, 1985 and 1990," *Alcohol Health & Research World* 18(1), 1994

To counter the cultural pressures on children to start drinking, Choice Three supporters also call for expanding educational programs and making them more sophisticated. Fatal Vision: A Lab for Life is one program that requires students to wear a special set of goggles that distorts perception the way alcohol does. In Providence, Rhode Island, for example, Coventry High School distributed goggles to students in a health class and asked them to ride scooters through an obstacle course. "There was like three of everything, and I felt dizzy," said Kerri Hachadorian, 16, after crashing into cardboard cutouts of a dog, a tree, and a stop sign. Frank Kuras, 18, said, "I think everybody should learn from it. It's a pretty good lesson."

> **An 11-year-old girl's impression of drinking alcohol: "It's like it's really cool. And I want to do it, too!"**

Fatal Vision goggles, shown here, are used in schools to give young people a sense of the potentially fatal difficulties they would have on the road after drinking.

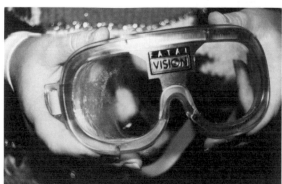

In Support

✓ Americans stopped smoking in huge numbers only after learning, really learning, that cigarettes were addictive and lethal. Similarly, Americans are very likely to stop abusing alcohol when they learn, really learn, that alcohol can be addictive and lethal.

✓ As Americans took to heart information about the ill effects of smoking, they developed new social norms for when and how people smoked. This is the successful model society can use to change unhealthy drinking habits.

✓ Alcohol abuse remains a major problem largely because society presents a highly positive picture of drinking and gives only lip service to its problems.

✓ Many Americans don't realize the damage alcohol does. For example, government research indicates that four in ten Americans do not know that alcohol can cause birth defects.

✓ Antidrug programs in schools focus too little attention on the drug alcohol, which causes more deaths and injuries than all illegal drugs combined.

✓ The alcohol industry should not exploit the youth market. As it is, students in eleventh and twelfth grades annually consume an estimated 1.1 billion cans of beer and 35 percent of all wine cooler products, according to a 1991 government study.

✓ Society supports alcohol advertising by making it a tax-deductible business expense. Eliminating this tax advantage would raise about $300 million annually in taxes and reduce alcohol advertising by 15 percent – which, in turn, would result in 1,300 fewer highway fatalities each year, according to government-sponsored research in 1997.

In Opposition

✗ This choice oversimplifies the problems of alcohol abuse by saying they can be vanquished by education. As it is, Americans with the most education, those on college campuses, do the most drinking.

✗ Education is a strategy for prevention, but education cannot help the millions of people who suffer from the disease of alcoholism.

✗ The problems of smoking are not at all similar to those of alcohol, and the solutions have to be different as well. This choice errs by portraying alcohol in an almost entirely negative way; what's needed are cultural changes that promote a positive model for the healthy use of alcohol.

✗ Laws are the most effective educators. For example, raising the legal drinking age to 21 from 18 continues to prevent thousands of traffic fatalities. Intentional or not, this choice takes the first steps in another doomed effort toward Prohibition by calling for such measures as restricting alcohol ads.

✗ Alcohol abuse is a very old problem, older even than advertising and marketing.

✗ This choice presumes that advertising furthers alcohol abuse, but the connection between advertising and drinking is not well understood. In a 1997 summary of research, the government reported that studies have not found an unqualified connection between alcohol advertising and alcohol consumption.

✗ This choice would increase taxes on alcoholic beverages, which would have the most economic impact on low-income people as well as on moderate drinkers who derive a health benefit from drinking.

For Further Reading / Educate for Societal Change

■ Debra F. Erenberg and George A. Hacker, "Last Call for High Risk Bar Promotions That Target College Students: A Community Action Guide," Washington, D.C.: Center for Science in the Public Interest, July 1997.

■ Deborah Saathoff, "Anti-Drug Efforts That Teach Life Skills Touted as Effective," *Dallas Morning News,* May 13, 1997.

■ http://www.faceproject.org is the Web site for FACE, Facing Alcohol Concerns through Education, which provides information and training materials for educators, as well as a set of "low-risk consumption guidelines" for responsible alcohol use.

Niculae Asciu

Enforce, Treat, or Educate?

At the University of Richmond, 13 percent of students report having been exploited sexually after heavy drinking. At Vanderbilt University, surveyed students said it was "common" for undergraduates to seek emergency room treatment for alcohol poisoning and injuries incurred while drunk.

The big picture looks equally grim: national studies report that four out of ten students drink in binges and that heavy drinking is a significant factor in academic failure, dropping out, vandalism, violence, injuries, and many deaths.

Nowhere else in America is the problem of alcohol abuse as concentrated as it is on the college campus. What can be done about it? The choices outlined in this issue book may overlap in certain aspects, but each choice speaks for one set of American priorities and views and, as the following summaries suggest, advocates a unique and consistent approach:

Choice One supporters: Student drinking has gotten out of control largely because authorities let it happen, through lax enforcement of laws governing the sale and use of alcohol. For example, more than a third of college students admit to driving while intoxicated, but only 1.4 percent say they have been arrested for drunk driving, according to a 1996 study conducted at Southern Illinois University's Core Institute. Strict law enforcement can turn this problem around, as demonstrated by police in Washtenaw County, Michigan, home of the University of Michigan. Immediately after stepping up arrests of drunk drivers and focusing on bars catering to students, these bars responded with a dramatic 300 percent increase in their refusal of alcohol to apparently intoxicated persons, according to a 1994 study published in the *Journal of Accident Analysis and Prevention.* Choice One supporters say society can reduce

Niculae Asciu

alcohol abuse by strictly enforcing alcohol control laws with the kind of speed, certainty, and severity that has proven highly effective in deterring alcohol offenses.

Choice Two supporters: Alcohol abuse is a health epidemic on campus that can be reduced only with medical intervention, not law enforcement. Early intervention is needed, as half of college binge drinkers also binged in high school, according to a 1994–1995 study done at Harvard University School of Public Health. What's needed, say supporters, is a comprehensive public health response that includes more medical research, treatment, and prevention programs for young people. All physicians, for example, should screen children and adolescents for alcohol use and abuse and offer medical advice and referrals for treatment, as per the recommendations of leading medical associations. Health insurers should cover these medical costs, much as they do other forms of healthcare. Many colleges are taking positive steps. The University of Maryland, for instance, has set up a Web site that provides students with materials to make a confidential assessment of their drinking problems and obtain information about counseling and treatment.

Choice Three supporters: Alcohol control laws and alcohol treatment will continue producing unsatisfactory results in college communities – primarily because alcohol laws lack public support and physicians tend to see only a limited role for themselves in reducing alcohol abuse. A fresh approach is needed, and a proven one is on hand: the societywide educational effort that helps young people realize that smoking isn't cool, sexy, or healthy. This national campaign has generated popular social norms and public policies for the responsible use, sale, and marketing of tobacco – and the same can be done with alcohol. It's easy to see why students got the wrong idea about drinking when popular culture and campus communities are filled with alcohol promotions. Up until now most colleges have ignored a 1990 appeal, made by the National Commission on Drug-Free Schools, to ban all alcohol advertising in school newspapers, at stadiums, and at all school events. When students start demanding these sorts of bans, alcohol abuse will decline.

Comparing the Choices

With one in four Americans affected by alcohol problems and nearly one in ten adults disabled by them, alcohol abuse remains one of the nation's most difficult social problems. How can a democratic society ensure safe use of a product that is both a civilized food and an addictive drug, one used legally by 100 million adults and used illegally by 11 million under the age of 21? To stimulate deliberation, the three approaches described in this issue book are summarized on these pages.

Choice I

Demand Citizen Responsibility

Most Americans drink alcohol responsibly and want others to comply with alcohol control laws, too. More people will comply with laws that clearly define irresponsible behavior and are enforced with certainty, speed, and severity.

What Can Be Done?

- Strengthen alcohol control laws to deter irresponsible drinking that harms others.

- Substantially increase law enforcement, providing for rapid, certain, and severe punishment.

- Give a higher priority in the nation's antidrug campaign to controlling alcohol, which is an illegal drug for minors.

In Support

- Americans have a right to drink alcohol responsibly and a right to be protected from those who don't.

- Laws that provide rapid, certain, and severe punishment are effective in deterring criminal abuse of alcohol.

- The nation's failure to adequately enforce alcohol control laws makes a mockery of them and encourages violations.

In Opposition

- This choice calls for intensifying an existing approach that isn't producing satisfactory results.

- Alcohol abuse is primarily a public health problem, not a law enforcement problem.

- Compliance with new laws would be no better than with old laws — until there is more agreement about the appropriate use of alcohol.

A Likely Tradeoff?

- In calling for stricter laws and enforcement to reduce alcohol abuse, this choice gives courts and police more power and, inevitably, reduces individual rights.

Choice 2

Treat the Public Health Epidemic

Abuse of alcohol is not a law enforcement problem, but a public health epidemic that the practice of medicine can best address. Laws can't stop an epidemic, but more research, prevention, and treatment can.

What Can Be Done?

- Substantially increase funding for research, prevention, and treatment programs; also expand health insurance coverage for alcohol problems.

- Have physicians counsel all patients — young and old — about alcohol use and abuse.

- Encourage all medical schools to provide courses in the problems of alcohol abuse.

In Support

- Alcohol abuse destroys the health of millions, yet the epidemic rages on, largely ignored and untreated.

- The American Medical Association recognized alcoholism as a disease in 1955, yet relatively few medical schools teach courses on treatment.

- The U.S. Department of Health and Human Services states unequivocally that treatment for alcohol problems is effective and recovery is possible for many.

In Opposition

- Many physicians and medical schools consider alcohol abuse a bad habit.

- Saying alcoholics are hapless victims of a disease ignores their decision to drink and undermines their willpower to stop abusing alcohol.

- No treatment program prevents relapses into irresponsible drinking, and only laws can deter irresponsible behavior.

A Likely Tradeoff?

- By focusing on research, prevention, and treatment, this choice would cost a lot and might take a long time to show results.

Choice 3

Educate for Societal Change

Society can't reduce alcohol abuse until Americans personally confront the problem — much the way they did with smoking. Societywide educational efforts, modeled on antismoking campaigns, could curb alcohol abuse.

What Can Be Done?

- Publicize the effects of alcohol abuse on health, families, crime, and careers.

- Insist that the liquor industry reinstitute its voluntary ban on advertising; expand the advertising ban to cover all alcohol products.

- Pressure the entertainment media to stop glamorizing alcohol and to start portraying alcohol use accurately.

In Support

- When Americans really confront the costs of alcohol abuse – the way they confronted the costs of smoking – the nation's alcohol problems will decline.

- Alcohol abuse remains a huge problem largely because alcohol is portrayed in such a positive manner in our society.

- Surveys show that many Americans don't know how harmful alcohol is; what's needed is education.

In Opposition

- The problems of smoking are not at all similar to those of alcohol abuse, and the solutions must differ as well.

- Laws are the best educational devices ever invented.

- Alcohol abuse is a very old health problem, older than advertising or television.

A Likely Tradeoff?

- In promoting an entirely negative view of alcohol, this choice might result in more restrictions on drinking than many Americans want.

What Are the National Issues Forums?

National Issues Forums bring together citizens around the nation to discuss challenging social and political issues of the day. They have addressed issues such as the economy, education, healthcare, foreign affairs, poverty, and crime.

Thousands of civic, service, and religious organizations, as well as libraries, high schools, and colleges, have sponsored forums. The sponsoring organizations select topics from among each year's most pressing public concerns, then design and coordinate their own forum programs, which are held through the fall, winter, and spring.

A different kind of talk

No two forums are alike. They range from small study circles to large gatherings modeled after town meetings, but all are different from everyday conversations and adversarial debates.

Since forums seek to increase understanding of complicated issues, participants need not start out with detailed knowledge of an issue. Forum organizers distribute issue books such as this one, featuring a nonpartisan overview of an issue and a choice of several public responses. By presenting each issue in a nonpartisan way, forums encourage participants to take a fresh look at the issues and at their own convictions.

In the forums, participants share their opinions, their concerns, and their knowledge. With the help of moderators and the issue books, participants weigh several possible ways for society to address a problem. They analyze each choice, the arguments for and against it, and the tradeoffs and other implications of the choice. Moderators encourage participants, as they gravitate to one option or another, to examine their basic values as individuals and as community members.

The search for common ground

Forums enrich participants' thinking on public issues. Participants confront each issue head-on, make an informed decision about how to address it, and come to terms with the likely consequences of their choices. In this deliberative process, participants often accept choices that are not entirely consistent with their individual wishes

and that impose costs they had not initially considered. This happens because the forum process helps people see issues from different points of view; participants use discussion to discover, not persuade or advocate. The best deliberative forums can help participants move toward shared, stable, well-informed public judgments about important issues.

Participants may hold sharply different opinions and beliefs, but in the forums they discuss their attitudes, concerns, and convictions about each issue and, as a group, seek to resolve their conflicting priorities and principles. In this way, participants move from making individual choices to making choices as members of a community – the kinds of choices from which public action may result.

Building community through public deliberation

In a democracy, citizens must come together to find answers they can all live with – while

NATIONAL ISSUES FORUMS

acknowledging that individuals have differing opinions. Forums help people find the areas where their interests and goals overlap. This allows a public voice to emerge that can give direction to public policy.

The forums are nonpartisan and do not advocate a particular solution to any public issue, nor should they be confused with referenda or public opinion polls. Rather, the forums enable diverse groups of Americans to determine together what direction they want policy to take, what kinds of action and legislation they favor and what, for their common good, they oppose.

Moving to action

Forums can lead to several kinds of public action. Generally, a public voice emerges in the results of the forums, and that helps set the government's compass, since forum results are shared with elected officials each year. Also, as a result of attending forums, individuals and groups may decide individually or with others to help remedy a public problem through citizen actions outside of government.

Alcohol
Controlling the Toxic Spill

One of the reasons people participate in the National Issues Forums is that they want leaders to know how they feel about the issues. So that we can present your thoughts and feelings about the issue, we'd like you to fill out this questionnaire before you attend forum meetings (or before you read this book, if you buy it elsewhere) and to fill out a second questionnaire after the forum (or after you've read the material). Before answering any of the questions, make up a three-digit number and write it in the box below.

The moderator of your local forum will ask you to hand in this questionnaire at the end of the session. If you are not attending a forum, send the completed questionnaire to National Issues Forums Research, 100 Commons Road, Dayton, Ohio 45459-2777.

Fill in your three-digit number here.

1. Here is a list of principles on which policies on controlling alcohol abuse might be based. How important do you think each one is?

	Very important	Somewhat important	Not at all important	Not sure
a. We should hold people responsible for the harm they cause when they drink.	☐	☐	☐	☐
b. We should treat alcohol abuse as a health problem rather than a crime.	☐	☐	☐	☐
c. Society must stop accepting, and even glamorizing, irresponsible drinking.	☐	☐	☐	☐
d. Programs that prevent alcohol abuse and treat alcoholism are much cheaper and more effective than prisons.	☐	☐	☐	☐
e. Education about the dangers of alcohol must start in the popular media.	☐	☐	☐	☐
f. We need to make and enforce stronger laws to control alcohol abuse.	☐	☐	☐	☐

2. Look at the list in Question #1 again. How strongly is each principle actually reflected in our current policies?

	Strongly	Somewhat strongly	Not at all	Not sure
a. We should hold people responsible for the harm they cause when they drink.	☐	☐	☐	☐
b. We should treat alcohol abuse as a health problem rather than a crime.	☐	☐	☐	☐
c. Society must stop accepting, and even glamorizing, irresponsible drinking.	☐	☐	☐	☐
d. Programs that prevent alcohol abuse and treat alcoholism are much cheaper and more effective than prisons.	☐	☐	☐	☐
e. Education about the dangers of alcohol must start in the popular media.	☐	☐	☐	☐
f. We need to make and enforce stronger laws to control alcohol abuse.	☐	☐	☐	☐

3. Are there any other principles that you think should guide public policy about controlling alcohol abuse? Please explain.

_____

_____

_____

4. How concerned are you about the issues listed below?

	Very concerned	Somewhat concerned	Not at all concerned	Not sure
a. Laws against drunk driving are too lax.	☐	☐	☐	☐
b. There are too few alcohol treatment programs for people who need them.	☐	☐	☐	☐
c. TV and movies reflect a society where excess drinking is cool.	☐	☐	☐	☐
d. Many people are unclear as to when drinking becomes risky.	☐	☐	☐	☐
e. Unless prisons provide treatment programs, jailed alcoholics are likely to commit more crimes when they come out.	☐	☐	☐	☐
f. Existing alcohol control laws often lack adequate enforcement.	☐	☐	☐	☐

5. Do you have any other concerns about policy concerning alcohol abuse? Please explain.

_____

_____

_____

6. How do you feel about these approaches to making policy about the control of alcohol abuse?

	Favor	Oppose	Not sure
a. Lower the legal blood alcohol limit for drunk driving EVEN IF this might make criminals out of ordinary Americans who are not a danger to society.	☐	☐	☐
b. Alcoholism and alcohol abuse should be treated as health problems, not crimes, EVEN IF that gives many people an excuse for antisocial behavior.	☐	☐	☐
c. Prevent alcohol abuse through major education programs EVEN IF this will not help millions of people who are already addicts.	☐	☐	☐

7. Which statement best describes how you feel? (Please mark only one answer.)

a. I am not at all certain what our public policy should be with regard to controlling alcohol abuse. ☐

b. I have a general sense of what our public policy should be. ☐

c. I have a definite opinion of what our public policy should be. ☐

8. Are you male or female? ☐ Male ☐ Female

9. How much schooling have you completed?

☐ Less than 6th grade ☐ 6th–8th grade ☐ Some high school ☐ High school graduate

☐ Some college ☐ College graduate ☐ Graduate school

10. Are you:

☐ White ☐ African American ☐ Hispanic ☐ Asian American ☐ Other (specify)

_____

11. How old are you?

☐ 17 or younger ☐ 18–29 ☐ 30–49 ☐ 50–64 ☐ 65 or older

12. Have you attended an NIF forum before? ☐ Yes ☐ No

13. If you answered "yes" to #12, how many forums have you attended? ☐ 1–3 ☐ 4–6 ☐ 7 or more

14. Do you live in the:

☐ Northeast ☐ South ☐ Midwest ☐ West

☐ Southwest ☐ Other

15. What is your ZIP code? _____

Alcohol
Controlling the Toxic Spill

Now that you've had a chance to read the book or attend a forum discussion, we'd like to know what you think about this issue. Your opinions, along with those of thousands of others who participated in this year's forums, will be reflected in a summary report prepared for participants as well as elected officials and policymakers working on this problem. Since we're interested in whether you have changed your mind about certain aspects of this issue, the questions are the same as those you answered earlier. Before answering the questions, please write in the box below the same three-digit number you used for the Pre-Forum Questionnaire.

Please hand this questionnaire to the forum leader at the end of the session, or mail it to: National Issues Forums Research, 100 Commons Road, Dayton, Ohio 45459-2777.

Fill in your three-digit number here.

1. Here is a list of principles on which policies on controlling alcohol abuse might be based. How important do you think each one is?

	Very important	Somewhat important	Not at all important	Not sure
a. We should hold people responsible for the harm they cause when they drink.	☐	☐	☐	☐
b. We should treat alcohol abuse as a health problem rather than a crime.	☐	☐	☐	☐
c. Society must stop accepting, and even glamorizing, irresponsible drinking.	☐	☐	☐	☐
d. Programs that prevent alcohol abuse and treat alcoholism are much cheaper and more effective than prisons.	☐	☐	☐	☐
e. Education about the dangers of alcohol must start in the popular media.	☐	☐	☐	☐
f. We need to make and enforce stronger laws to control alcohol abuse.	☐	☐	☐	☐

2. Look at the list in Question #1 again. How strongly is each principle actually reflected in our current policies?

	Strongly	Somewhat strongly	Not at all	Not sure
a. We should hold people responsible for the harm they cause when they drink.	☐	☐	☐	☐
b. We should treat alcohol abuse as a health problem rather than a crime.	☐	☐	☐	☐
c. Society must stop accepting, and even glamorizing, irresponsible drinking.	☐	☐	☐	☐
d. Programs that prevent alcohol abuse and treat alcoholism are much cheaper and more effective than prisons.	☐	☐	☐	☐
e. Education about the dangers of alcohol must start in the popular media.	☐	☐	☐	☐
f. We need to make and enforce stronger laws to control alcohol abuse.	☐	☐	☐	☐

3. Are there any other principles that you think should guide public policy about controlling alcohol abuse? Please explain.

_____

_____

_____

4. How concerned are you about the issues listed below?

	Very concerned	Somewhat concerned	Not at all concerned	Not sure
a. Laws against drunk driving are too lax.	☐	☐	☐	☐
b. There are too few alcohol treatment programs for people who need them.	☐	☐	☐	☐
c. TV and movies reflect a society where excess drinking is cool.	☐	☐	☐	☐
d. Many people are unclear as to when drinking becomes risky.	☐	☐	☐	☐
e. Unless prisons provide treatment programs, jailed alcoholics are likely to commit more crimes when they come out.	☐	☐	☐	☐
f. Existing alcohol control laws often lack adequate enforcement.	☐	☐	☐	☐

5. Do you have any other concerns about policy concerning alcohol abuse? Please explain.

    _____

    _____

    _____

6. How do you feel about these approaches to making policy about the control of alcohol abuse?

	Favor	Oppose	Not sure
a. Lower the legal blood alcohol limit for drunk driving EVEN IF this might make criminals out of ordinary Americans who are not a danger to society.	☐	☐	☐
b. Alcoholism and alcohol abuse should be treated as health problems, not crimes, EVEN IF that gives many people an excuse for antisocial behavior.	☐	☐	☐
c. Prevent alcohol abuse through major education programs EVEN IF this will not help millions of people who are already addicts.	☐	☐	☐

7. Which statement best describes how you feel? (Please mark only one answer.)

    a. I am not at all certain what our public policy should be with regard to controlling alcohol abuse. ☐

    b. I have a general sense of what our public policy should be. ☐

    c. I have a definite opinion of what our public policy should be. ☐

8. Are there any other comments you would like to make about U.S. policy on this issue? Please explain.

    _____

    _____

    _____

9. What is your ZIP code? _____